IBIZA &
FORMENTERA

Editorial Everest would like to thank you for purchasing this book. It has been created by an extensive and complete publishing team made up of photographers, illustrators and authors specialised in the field of tourism, together with our modern cartography department. Everest guarantees that the contents of this work were completely up to date at the time of going to press, and we would like to invite yoy to send us any information that helps us to improve our publications, so that we may always offer QUALITY TOURISM.

QUALITY
TOURISM
WITH
EVEREST

Please send your comments to:
Editorial Everest. Dpto. de Turismo
Apartado 339 – 24080 León (Spain)
Or e-mail them to us at turismo@everest.es

Editorial Management: Raquel López Varela

Editorial coordination: Eva María Fernández

Text: Juan Pérez Escribano

Photographs: Juan Pérez, Georama and Archivo Everest

Diagrams: José Manuel Núñez

Cover design: Alfredo Anievas

Digital image processing: David Aller and Ángel Rodríguez

Translation: EURO:TEXT

© EDITORIAL EVEREST, S. A.
Carretera León-La Coruña, km 5 - LEÓN
ISBN: 84-241-0614-8
Legal deposit: LE. 234 - 2006
Printed in Spain

EDITORIAL EVERGRÁFICAS, S. L.
Carretera León-La Coruña, km 5
LEÓN (Spain)

IBIZA &
FORMENTERA

The **Pitiusas Islands** (the group of islands which includes Ibiza and Formentera, amongst others) are located approximately 90 miles off Spain's east coast, with the town of Denia being the closest point on the mainland, just 56 miles from the port of San Antonio, on the island's southwest coast. Towards the northeast, it stands 45 miles from the island of Mallorca and 150 miles from Barcelona.

The island of Ibiza covers an area of 572 km², making it the third largest in the Balearic archipelago, and the island of Formentera measures 82 km² and stands 10 miles from the port of Ibiza. Other small islands which surround the coastline include Es Vedrá, Es Vedranell, Espalmador, Tagomago, Espardell, Illa Plana, Illa des Bosc, Sa Conillera and Margalida.

Es Vedrá.

The island's coastline consists of high cliffs in the northeast, from Cala Llosá (Punta Galera), famous for being one of the first nudist enclaves back in the sixties, to the town of Santa Eulalia, although natural gullies have been formed between the mountains which make it possible to reach the sea via green pine forests, alongpathways which lead to small, almost untouched coves where Ibizan fishermen still store their fishing vessels in dry dock-huts built between the rocks, on the edge of the sea, enabling them to fish every day if the winds are favourable. Some of these coves are only accessible on foot and others may only be reached in 4-wheel drive vehicles.

The rest of the coastline from Santa Eulalia to the city of Ibiza stands at sea level, however it becomes steep again, whilst maintaining easy access to the sea, in the town of San José, where the island's most beautiful sandy beaches begin, such as Cala Tarida, Cala Vadella, Cala Conta and Cala Bassa, whose geographical orientation means that they offer wonderful sunsets.

The beaches of Ibiza have recently become more than a combination of sand to lie on and sea to swim in. They are unique and unbeatable places for leisure and relaxation, where you can enjoy a delicious breakfast at dawn or the most romantic evening at nightfall, surrounded by all-encompassing "made in Ibiza" sounds and the most exquisite delicacies, accompanied by exotic drinks that just do not taste the same anywhere else. If we must "criticise" these worldly pleasures, it would be to say that, whilst not being luxury items, they are not within the reach of all budgets, since the problem of overcrowding is prevented by means of prices which are themselves selective. Yet this only serves to make them all the more "desirable", so much so that they have become

Previous double page, Cala Carbó.

Rails for storing "llauds" in dry dock-huts.

Above, Ses Boques (Es Cubells).   Below, Cala Saona (Formentera).

popular among the "jet-set" and famous people from all over the world. Nonetheless, we must stress, without giving any names, that this is only true of a few specific beaches which have decided to offer this option to a certain set of visitors who have chosen the island as their preferred holiday resort.

Most of the island's beaches opt for the natural pleasures of the sun and the sea. They offer all kinds of water sports and boat trips in order to build up the visitor's appetite and make them unable to resist a good *bullit de peix* (fish stew) or grilled Ibizan rock fish at one of the many restaurant-stands that are to be found on the beaches.

Each beach or cove has its own charm because of the unique character of its sand or pebbles, the colour and transparency of its waters, the pine trees at the edge of the sea… Benirrás, Cala d'hort, Cala Salada, Cala Carbó, Pou des Lleó and so on, up to almost one hundred

coves, beaches and hideaways where the sea will create your very own private beach.

The indigenous plant life consists mainly of large pine forests which, when seen from above, appear to cover the entire surface of the island, forming a green blanket only marked by hundreds of white dots which correspond to rural cottages, of a beautifully simple and restrained design.

This is also accompanied by many other trees which are more typical of cultivated areas: fig, carob, almond and olive trees which blossom early due to the climate. It is not uncommon to see the valleys of Santa Inés and San Mateo in blossom in January or February, providing a view which is relaxing in all senses. Savins and low bushes fill the areas that are not occupied by pine trees, above all in areas close to the sea. As one heads inland, the soil becomes red and rich in minerals and during the early spring, the countryside

Endemic lizard and Ibizan Hound.

House entrance, Sant Joan.

Wild irises and prickly pears flourish on the island.

forms a rainbow of flowers which cannot fail to delight photographers and nature-lovers. Due to their rarity, special mention must also be given to approximately twenty species of orchids that grow on the island.

In the sea, of particular interest are the extensive meadows of Posidonia sea grass, a plant which is endemic to the Mediterranean.

Ibizan fauna is also highly valuable with its lizards, hedgehogs, genets, wild rabbits, different insects, sea birds, falcons, owls, poultry and farm animals. Special mention must be given to the Ibizan Hound, a breed of dog that is related to a mythical animal from Ancient Egypt.

There are lizards which are unique to the species and strangely vary in colour, depending upon the part of the island in which they live: green, bluish, black or brown.

For some years now, colonies of flamingos have settled in the Ses Salines Nature Reserve, not wanting to continue their flight towards Southern Spain or Africa as they used to, since they find sufficient food on the island.

Over the course of time, fishing has almost exhausted the indigenous coastal species such as "raó", scorpion fish, grouper, octopus and Dublin Bay prawns, amongst others.

THE CITY OF IBIZA (EIVISSA)

The city of **Ibiza** was founded in the year 654 BC and was called *Ibusim (Ibshm)* by the Carthaginians, in reference to Bes, one of their gods. During its long history, it has been invaded (although not always occupied) by various different nations (Greeks, Romans, Vandals, Byzantines, Arabs, Normans, Almoravids, Almohads, Turks, Algerian pirates, etc.) and was defended for many years by our closest privateering ancestors, including Antonio Riquer, who was from Ibiza itself. As a result, the islanders have a great mixture of cultures in their genes and this has given them a special and unique ability to welcome all kinds of visitors with open arms, without recalling or resenting any of the invasions suffered.

The Greeks used to refer to this group of islands as the *Pitiusas* because of the pine forests that grow on them.

In 1235, the troops of the Archbishop of Tarragona, Guillem de Montgrí, conquered the islands and incorporated them within the Kingdom of Aragon.

Ibiza port.

Monument to Vara de Rey (Eivissa).

Dalt Vila.

Also called *Ebusus* by the Romans and *Yebisah* by the Arabs, modern-day **Eivissa** is a city divided into three different urban areas. The **upper city** *(Dalt Vila)*, declared a *World Heritage Site* in 2000, stands inside walled grounds. **The marina and the La Peña** *(Sa Penya)* district are to be found between the outside of the aforesaid walls and the port, where fishing activities continued until just a few years ago, when the first tourist boats began to arrive. Lastly, **El Ensanche** *(Eixample)* is the new part of the city which is being extended towards the town of Jesús, past the sailing club, marinas, Talamanca beach and Botafoc dock (recently extended to accommodate large liners) on one side, towards Santa Eulalia on the other and towards San Rafael to the southwest, thereby creating a large industrial estate, and towards San José, along the beaches of Ses Figueretes, Playa den Bossa and San Jordi and past the airport.
Inside the walled city, or Dalt Vila, we can find Ibiza's main artistic assets, although it is indeed a monument in itself, formed by narrow and well-preserved alleyways housing many craft stores, clothes shops, art galleries and restaurants, mixed with unusual houses, some of which have been converted into charming little hotels in which one can feel part of history, staying where the Roman Curia or rich Moors once had their homes.
The **Cathedral of Santa María** de las Nieves, a Gothic building from the 13th and 14th centuries which was modified and extended in the 18th century, was constructed on the site of a former Muslim mosque. Of the original Gothic building, one may still see the bell tower, the apse chapels and the door of the antesacristy. The rest corresponds to 18th century reforms, except for the high altar which dates from the 19th century. The former Casa de la Curia (currently part of the Bishop's Palace) features a Gothic-style doorway and is to be found in the Cathedral square, at the exit which leads to Calle Mayor.

Next to the Cathedral stands the Archaeological Museum, which is considered to have one of the most comprehensive and important collections of Punic art in the world. The museum is located in the building which first housed the University and later, until 1838, the Town Hall. It contains a large number of small pieces found in various excavations, with particularly interesting representations of the Punic goddess *Tanit* and the Carthaginian god *Bes*.

The **Convent of Santo Domingo,** built between the 14th and 17th centuries, features slender tile-covered domes. 19th century fresco paintings decorate the inner vault, however they are now in a poor condition due to fire damage. It is also worth noting the altarpiece of the Chapel of the Rosario.

Adjacent to the Church of Santo Domingo, within the convent grounds, stands the ancient Dominican Convent of San Vicente Ferrer, the current seat of the City Council. The ancient cloisters are now used for classical music recitals and cultural events.

The highest part of the Dalt Vila contains the so-called **Castle,** a building which dates from the Muslim period and has undergone subsequent modifications. Negotiations are well underway to convert it into a *Parador Nacional* (top-class state-owned hotel). It is protected by the fortresses of Sant Bernat and Sant Jordi, strategic defence points from which the troops of Guillem de Montgrí began their conquest, with the blessing of King Jaime I.

Fortress.

14

A second walled enclosure was built in the 16th century under the rule of Carlos V and was completed under Felipe II. It has seven fortresses and is reached via the Portal de las Tablas which is flanked by two headless Roman statues and crowned with the coat of arms of the Hapsburg dynasty, with an inscription which indicates the date of completion of the walled enclosure (1585), under the rule of Felipe II. From left to right, the first fortress is that of *Sant Joan (San Juan)*, which was intended to protect the La Marina district and the port. This is followed by *Santa Llúcia* in the Sa Penya district, Santa Tecla in an area of cliffs and *Sant Bernat* and *San Jordi* on the defence line of *Es Sot*. From *Sant Jaime*, the Punic necropolis of *Puig del Molins* can be seen, with more than 3000 Punic and Roman tombs which now form part of the **Museum of Puig del Molins.** On this site, not only were a large number of small items, terracotta pieces, masks, amulets and sacred urns found but also the aforementioned figures of the goddess *Tanit* and the god *Bes*. Lastly, we have the *Portal Nou* fortress, at another entrance to the walled enclosure.

Above, Ibiza Cathedral.

Below, market.

Playa de Figueretas.

Playa de Talamanca.

IBIZAN NIGHTS

Many visitors miss the beauty of the island because they devote their time to enjoying the nightlife. This is comprehensible, because Ibiza provides options which are difficult to refuse.

Beyond the distorted image of a place in which, for some, "everything goes" (the more extravagant the better), Ibizan nights are as diverse and special as they are enriching and unique.

After returning from the beach at dusk and dressing in "casually smart" clothes, there is such a wide choice of restaurants and leisure activities that it is impossible to enjoy them all in one short holiday. If you choose Ibiza city, before dining you can take a stroll around the port, wandering between craft stalls, among a mixture of people who will remind you of the hippy Ibiza of the 60's, since most of them practice and maintain the same spirit.

If you are a romantic at heart and enjoy watching the sun set, you should head for San Antonio, where you can spend unforgettable moments, filling your spirit with fresh energy and listening to well-chosen music in one of the countless outdoor cafés that are to be found on the sea edge. This would provide an ideal appetiser before filling your stomach with a delicious dinner in any of the many local restaurants.

However, if you like to enjoy moonlit walks surrounded by peace and quiet, take a walk along the Santa Eulalia promenade and have dinner in one of its outdoor restaurants. Another alternative is to visit the small inland towns where it seems that time has stood still, such as Santa Inés, San Mateo, Santa Gertrudis, San Miguel, San Juan,

Inside Es Paradis nightclub.

San Carlos, San Rafael, San José, San Agustín, so many saints that you will feel obliged to give prayer in thanks for being there.

For night owls, the night has only just begun. There are so many pubs and so much nightlife on offer that different places come in and out of fashion each summer, although whichever you choose, you will not be disappointed.

Lastly, the rush for the world's most famous macro-clubs: Pachá, Space, Amnesia, Privilege, El Divino and Es Paradís, amongst others. These are shrines to music, where the most famous DJs play every summer. Each club has its own style and in the rest of the world they are seen as authentic "schools" for musical tendencies. There is a legend which says that the Greek muses of music spent their summers in Ibiza.

Special mention must be given to the international INJUVE jazz festival which is organised to coincide with the full moon at the end of July. It is held outdoors, in the incomparable setting of the Santa Lucía fortress, from which the entire city may be seen, under the protection of the Cathedral tower.

It is not unusual to go out one night to an unpretentious bar and find straightforward and down-to-earth musicians playing for those who are lucky enough to be there and to later discover that they were, in fact, established jazz players who live on the island, hidden from fame.

In fact, many artists, painters, sculptors and writers have discovered the peace and inspiration that float in the island's air and have decided to live here.

DJ in Pachá nightclub.

Sant Antoni, from
Sa Talaia.

Sant Antoni de Portmany (San Antonio Abad)

Sant Antoni is located 15 km from the capital city of Ibiza, on the western side of the island. It has 16,000 inhabitants in the main town and approximately 25,000 in the entire municipality. The Romans named its beautiful bay *Portus Magnus*. This is a natural inlet which has been reduced, with the passing of time, by the construction of a promenade which practically surrounds it. It was ransacked and destroyed by Turkish pirates in 1383, when it was just a simple fishing village.

It is now a cosmopolitan town, full of hotels. Interestingly, most of the latter are located in the part of the bay that belongs to the neighbouring town of Sant Josep, which starts at *Es Pouet beach*, although this division is only effective in administrative terms since, geographically speaking, the hotels, restaurants, bars, stores and souvenir shops form a uniform line along the coast, as far as the beach of *Port des Torrent*.

The port was recently extended with the construction of a ferry station and maintains an exclusive service to Denia, which is a mere 56 miles away. It can be reached in just 2 hours on the new fast boats, compared to the standard 4-hour service which still operates.

Next to the aforesaid ferry station, there stands the *Sant Antoni Watersports Club*, which offers 350 berths, a sizeable sailing and canoeing club and also has plans for enlargement which are well underway.

Over recent years, a group of businessmen and the local council have been working to transfer and diversify what is called the *West End*, a busy tourist area of pubs and clubs in the centre of the town, to more suitable and spacious parts of the bay, so that the crowds of people and music are not all

concentrated in one place: one area towards *Ses Variadas* and *Caló del Moro beach,* another on the promenade of the beach itself and another in a quieter area in the old quarter, close to the church, with small bars where one normally encounters local inhabitants and less boisterous tourists. The Council also encourages groups of craftspeople and jazz musicians to gather in the square behind the church, thereby creating a small street market.

The local festivals take place on 17th January *(Feast Day of Sant Antoni)* and 24th August, *Feast Day of Saint Bartholomew,* who is, strangely, the Patron Saint of San Antoni.

The parish church, which is celebrating its 700th anniversary this year, is a beautiful temple with a defence tower that was built to resist pirate invasions.

The main attraction of Sant Antoni and its surroundings are the coves and beaches which have perhaps the finest sands and clearest waters. They are all easily accessible from land, however we would suggest taking one of the numerous and very safe boats which constantly depart from the promenade quayside. This will enable you to enjoy the sun, the sea and the beauty of the coastline whilst avoiding the problems of traffic and parking in the summer months.

The closest, such as *Port des Torrent, Cala Bassa, Cala Conta, Cala Gracio* and *Cala Saladda,* are just over half an hour away by boat, and even the more distant locations, such as *Cala Tarida, Cala Vadella* and

Illa Margarida (Sant Antoni).
Diving area.

Sa Punta des Molí
(Sant Antoni).

Left, Church
of Sant Antoni.

Cala Carbó, are never more than an hour away. To visit the more remote beaches you can arrange organised trips which will allow you to spend the day on the beach of your choice. There also exists a taxi-boat service which constantly crosses the bay, taking tourists to and from their hotels.

At dusk, the sunset-watching ritual has become an unmissable event for hundreds of people. Some prefer a quiet table, with a drink and *chill out* music in the background at

Llauds in Sant Antoni watersports club.

one of the many bars on the sea front, whilst many others opt for the pure simplicity of nature, sitting on the rocks or the sand with their feet in the water, listening to the sea and waiting for the orange-coloured sun to drop down and hide itself behind the horizon, disappearing into the water or vanishing behind **Conillera Island,** which stands opposite the bay.

If we leave Sant Antoni and head north towards *Santa Agnes,* turning off towards the *beach of Cala Salada* and continuing through thick pine woods for approximately five kilometres, we reach the cliffs of *Cap Nunó.* Here, a steep descent which can be problematic for vehicles takes us to the controversial *Cueva des Vi* (known as *Ses Fontanellas),* a small opening half way up the cliff, currently enclosed by railings, which contains somewhat deteriorated paintings that date from the Bronze Age. However, you can discover the real charm of the place by continuing the descent along more than 200 hand-

carved stone steps which will take you to another cave at the sea's edge which, according to local gossip, was the entry point for smugglers (of alcohol and tobacco, amongst other goods) in the not so distant past.

In this same direction, approximately 2 km outside Sant Antoni, we can also find an unusual unfinished church with unpainted stone walls called *Sa Capella.* It is said that religious services were never held in this church, which is currently a beautiful restaurant. Nearby, we find the Paleochristian Chapel of Santa Agnés, a tomb-like oratory found in the *Cave of Santa Agnés,* which has been declared a *National Monument.* It contains a presbytery and two side niches, despite measuring less than three metres deep and two metres high.

If we follow the road for approximately 8 km as it winds its way through the mountains, we will come to a plain *(Pla de Corona)* full of almond trees which will take us to Santa Agnés de Corona. This small town has a square with a pretty church and a couple of bars where the peaceful and traditional nature of the local country folk, combined with a delicious Spanish omelette, make any visit well worthwhile.

If we follow the path to the left of the square, we will reach some cliffs which have a magnificent view, with Margalida Island in the distance. From the right of the square, we continue along the road for a further 5 km, between cultivated fields and authentic rural cottages, to reach Sant Mateu d'Aubarca, another small country town with a church and several bars. The latter also tend to serve as the local store, post-office, restaurant and meeting place in these towns. We come close to the "frontier" with the municipality of Santa Eulalia before heading back towards Sant Antoni via the *Es Broll*, a gully used for crop-growing which has a network of irrigation channels dating from Arab times. Next we come to Buscatell, with its chapel and bar-shop which, in this case, also serves as an art gallery. In this land of rich red soils, 2 km away from Sant Antoni, we can find vineyards which have produced very interesting wines and have, together with another two of the island's wineries, requested that they be given the status of "Denomination of Origin" by the regional parliament. In order to finish our visit to the municipality of Sant Antoni, we must travel 8 km towards the city of Ibiza in order to reach the town of *Sant Rafel de Forca,* which contains a pretty church in pure Ibizan style, as well as the workshops of several well-known potters. This is a relaxing place for a pleasant evening out since it has a large number of restaurants.

Sunset in
Sa Conillera.

Almond trees in Santa Inés.

Playa de Port des Torrent.   Cala Salada.

Church of Santa Eulària.

SANTA EULARIA DES RIU

Santa Eulalia is located on the east side of the island, 15 km from the capital. It stands below a hill which is called *Puig de Missa* or "Mass Hill", because a church stands upon it, and on the banks of the Balearic Islands' only river, which normally contains very little water due to scarce rainfall.

The population of the town stands at around 16,000 and there are around 26,000 people in the municipality as a whole.

The parish church was built in 1568. Like others on the island, it consists of the temple itself plus a defence tower which was necessary due to the raids of Turkish and Algerian pirates that the island constantly suffered. A 14th century chapel existed previously on the same site but was destroyed by Turkish pirates.

The Ethnological Museum of Ibiza has been created next to the church and provides an interesting depiction of rural history and traditions, many of which still continue. Nearby, there is another small museum-gallery dedicated to the painter Laureano Barrau.

The new part of the town extends from the aforementioned hill to the sea, along the coast towards Es Canar on one side and towards Cala Llonga on the other. Most of the buildings in this area are tourist developments and hotels.

The sailing club, at the end of an extremely long promenade, has a capacity for 740 berths. The surrounding streets bustle with life, making it the centre of the town's leisure and shopping activities, together with an area located close to the Town Hall and the main street, Calle San Jaime.

The Roca Llisa Golf Club is located 4 km south, towards Ibiza and past

Cala Llonga. It has two courses (9 and 18 holes) and is the only place on the island where one can practice this sport.

If we continue along the same road, we reach the town of **Jesús,** close to the city of Ibiza, with the outstanding 15th century Parish Church of Nuestra Señora de Jesús and its valuable Gothic altarpiece. Towards the north, we come to another important tourist destination at *Playa de Es Canar.* For years, this has been famous for its hippy street market in *Punta Arabí,* where every Wednesday you can experience for a day the atmosphere and philosophy of the descendents of the *hippies* that arrived in the 60's, who make a living by selling their own creations, mostly craftwork, jewellery and Ibizan-style clothing.

If we continue along the coast, we come to magnificent beaches such as *Niu Blau, Cala Nova, Cala Llenya, Cala Mastella, Cala Boix, Pou des Lleó, Es Figueral* and *S'aigua Blanca.*

Most of them have their own dry docks where the local fishermen keep the "llaud" vessels that they use to fish each day, both to feed themselves and to supply the traditional restaurants that are to be found in each bay.

At the top of the small island of Tagomago (where an endemic lizard species lives, the *Podarcis pityusensis),* we find the 18th century *Torre de Companitx,* one of the many watchtowers that were built to warn the population of pirate attacks. All the towers on the island communicated with each other by means of a system of mirrors which reflected the sun, a kind of "luminary Morse code".

Leading inland, 4 km from Santa Eulalia, we find **Sant Carles de Peralta,** a quiet town with an 18th century double-arcaded church and another street market, no less famous than that of Punta Arabí, located in a landscaped precinct called *Las Dalias* which opens every Saturday.

Dry dock-hut.

Church of San Carlos.

Sa Caleta.

Above, Cap Llibrell. Below, Playa de Santa Eulària.

Cala Llonga.

Cala Jondal.

In the Cana Anneta bar, next to the church, the purest hippy atmosphere still survives with a mixture of locals and tourists which is reminiscent of the 60's and 70's when the island attracted the largest community of followers of the "make love not war" philosophy, a movement that was mainly created by young people who were against the Vietnam war.

Also inland, towards the west, we find **Santa Gertrudis de Fruitera,** a town which has undergone considerable growth in just a few years due to its strategic geographical position in the centre of the island, close to all locations. Furthermore, it has a very popular but laidback nightlife, with many bars and outdoor cafés surrounding its beautiful church, which possesses the largest bell tower on the island.

SANT JOSEP DE SA TALAIA

To the south, this is the largest municipality on the island. It extends along the coast from *Platja den Bossa,* a tourist resort linked to the extension of Ibiza city, to *Platja des Pouet,* in the bay of Sant Antoni. It is 15 km from Ibiza and 9 km from Sant Antoni and encompasses the parishes of *Sant Agustí des Vedrá, San Jordi de Ses Salines* and *San Francesc de S'Estany,* which total around 14,000 inhabitants.

The town centre and main street are located between the two sections of the road which link it with Ibiza, on the one side, and Sant Antoni, on the other.

The parish church, where all the neighbouring alleyways converge, dates from the 16th century. In pure Ibizan style, it has a reformed square which is used as the setting for cultural activities, traditional dances and musical concerts. Inside, the main altarpiece is of particular interest.

A couple of kilometres outside the town stands the highest point on Ibiza, **Sa Talaia,** at a height of 475 m, from which one can see practically the entire island and even, on clear days, the mountain range which runs along the coast of Denia.

Church of Sant Josep.

Flamingos in Ses Salines Nature Reserve.

If we follow the road towards Sant Antoni for 4 km, we will find the small town of **Sant Agustí des Vedrá,** a group of traditional rural houses which are gathered around a church and have remained unchanged over the years. A delightful spot. The church follows the typical Ibizan style of construction and is one of the few which does not include a vestibule or defence tower.

From Sant Agustí, we head to the left, between fields full of almond, olive and carob trees, towards the beaches that are preferred by hundreds of foreigners who have chosen Ibiza as their place of residence or retirement retreat.

From *Port des Torrent,* a beach close to Sant Antoni, along the coast to *Cala Bassa, Cala Conta, Cala Codolar, Cala Corral, Cala Tarida, Cala Molí, Cala Vedella, Cala Carbó, Cala D'hort, Cala Llentrisca, Ses Boques, Porroig, Es Yondal, Sa Caleta, Platja des Codolar, Platja de Ses Salines,* *Platja des Cavallet* and *Platja den Bossa,* they all make Sant Josep the municipality with the greatest number of tourist havens.

Standing in **Cala Conta,** a beach of crystal-clear waters and fine sands, we can see the islands called *Ses Bledas* opposite, next to S'Espartar, Illa des Bosc and the largest of them all, *Sa Conillera.* The Torre den Rovira, a watchtower built in 1763, stands at a distance of 300 metres from the beach.

Towards the south, the road links the beaches, skirting the natural gullies, full of pine trees, which flow into them, and is only interrupted near the cliffs of *Es Cubells* and after *Sa Caleta,* as it approaches the airport, where it is forced to detour around the *Ses Salines Nature Reserve.*

We leave behind us the beautiful, sandy beaches of Cala Tarida and Cala Vedella, full of luxurious houses, apartments and hotels, and turn away from the wild coastline to visit

Cala d'Hort, a magical place watched over by two islands, the majestic island of Es Vedrá and the smaller island of Es Vedranell, about which there exist all kinds of legends. From October onwards, their dusk light offers comfort to the soul.

Close to the cove, there exist the remains of an ancient Punic-Roman settlement called *Ses Paises de Cala d'Hort* which dates from between the 5th and 7th centuries AD.

From the beach, we can see the *Cap del Judeus* to the left, with a watchtower which is called the Torre des Savinar but is also known as the *Torre del Pirata* or Pirate's Tower. due to the name it was given by Vicente Blasco Ibáñez in his novel *Los Muertos Mandan*. The cliffs underneath the tower contain the remains of a Roman quarry, Sa Pedrera de Cala d'Hort, from which *marés,* a sedimentary limestone typical of the island, was extracted. Its clear-cut faces form small natural pools next to the sea which people have recently begun to call *Atlantis.* We continue towards Sa Caleta and find the remains of a site where, according to studies carried out, the first Phoenicians settled before founding the city of Ibiza, in the 7th century BC.

Leaving Es Codolar International Airport behind us, we come to **Sant Jordi de Ses Salines** and one of the most original Ibizan churches whose roof is surrounded by battlements to form a defensive wall, although ancient documents state that it once also had a defence tower.

After leaving Sant Jordi, we pass through **Sant Francesc,** which also has a simple church, and we enter the *Ses Salines Nature Reserve.* This area covers 400 hectares and has been used for salt extraction ever since the times of the Carthaginians and has been one of the island's main economic resources for many years now.

Next page, Cala d'Hort and Es Vedrá island.

Cala Vedella.

Mention must be given to the fact that every year, during Holy Week, an ancient boat race, called the Salt Route, is held between the peninsula and Ibiza to commemorate the crossings made by boats loaded with salt.

38 Ses Salines produces 80,000 metric tonnes per year and most of the salt is loaded at the small port of Sa Canal, at the end of Platja de Ses Salines. It is interesting to recall that the name of this substance gave rise to the word "salary", because in former times workers were paid with certain quantities of salt.

Another defence tower is to be found between *Platja de Ses Salines* and *Es Cavallet,* namely the Torre de Ses Portes. This was built by the same architect that built the new city walls in Ibiza, the Italian Giovanni Battista Calvi, who also constructed the *Torre de la Sal Rossa,* the next tower that we encounter as we head towards Platja den Bossa.

Cala de Sant Vicente.

SANT JOAN DE LABRITJA

The island's most northerly municipality is that of **Sant Joan,** at a distance of 22 km from Ibiza. It has around 6000 inhabitants distributed throughout a mainly agricultural valley and a mountainous area with extensive pine forests dotted with white country cottages. The parishes of Sant Llorenc de Balafia, Sant Miquel de Balanzat and Sant Vicent de Sa Cala form the municipality's other towns.

Its church is dedicated to the patron saint San Juan Bautista and dates from the 18th century, although the bell tower was added in 1900. The town is small and quiet and its slow growth has respected the architectural setting, giving the impression that time has stood still.

Approximately 4 km to the southwest stands *Sant Llorens de Balafia*, a small rural town which also possesses an 18th century church. At a distance of 500 metres stands the hamlet of Balafia, a group of seven houses and three towers which was used to defend the peasants against greatly-feared pirate raids.

After leaving Sant Joan and travelling 6 km along a windy road through pine woods, we reach *Sant Vicent de Sa Cala*, whose church was one of the last to be built on the island and is an example of Ibizan architecture. If we continue a further 6 km along the same road we come to *Cala de Sant Vicent*, a sandy beach surrounded by hotels, with Tagomago Island in the distance. Local boats provide access to the latter, offering relaxing trips which allow visitors to observe indigenous

fauna, such as cormorants, seagulls and an endemic species of lizard. Every October, a well-established rally is held from Sant Joan to Cala Sant Vicent which is called the *Baixada a Sa Cala (Descent to the Cove)* due to the spectacular nature of its curves.

In 1907, one of the most important Punic archaeology sites on the island, *Cueva des Cuieram,* was discovered just 2 km away from Sa Cala. Here, a shrine to the goddess *Tanit* was found, with objects and figures of worship which are now kept in the Archaeological Museum of Ibiza. Further to the north lies **Portinatx**, a group of several coves which was the refuge of fishermen before the large-scale arrival of tourists to the island. Its transparent waters and sandy beaches have made it one of the most highly-developed tourist resorts, with hotels right up to the sea front. Following the coast towards the west, we reach **Cala Xarraca**, which is almost entirely free of property developments due to its wild setting. It is watched over by another 18th century defence tower positioned on Punta Marés.

Other small coves exist along the entire length of the coast, such as Benirrás, which has become controversial of late due to crowds of people from all over the island (and even from abroad) who gather there when there is a full moon to sit on the beach and play tam tam drums throughout the night – an event which is considered to be highly participative and popular by some, annoying and disrespectful of the environment by others.

Before reaching the important tourist resort of Port de Sant Miquel, we can visit the natural grotto of *Can Marcá.* The port is sheltered by cliffs from which several hotels appear to almost "hang".

By following a steep road we reach *Sant Miquel de Balanzat,* a town that surrounds a small hill upon which there stands a church that dates from the 14th century, although it was not completed until the 17th century. Different to the island's other churches because of its courtyard and adjacent structures, it nonetheless maintains a fortress-like appearance and is considered the oldest in Ibiza.

Portinatx.

Balafia.

Church of Sant Joan.

FORMENTERA

The island of **Formentera** has a surface area of 115 km^2 and a population of around 5000 inhabitants. It is located to the south of Ibiza, at a distance of 11 miles from port to port and just 3 miles at the closest point. It is separated by the Straight of *Es Freís* and indicated by the small islands of *Es Penjats, Espardell, Espardelló* and *Espalmador.* The longest distance on the island measures 15 km and its highest point is La Mola, at an altitude of 202 m.

The climate is mild throughout the entire year, with little rainfall, and the island's vegetation mainly consists of savins and some areas of pine forest, although most were felled long ago to produce charcoal. Crops are limited to just a few fields of cereals and fruit trees typical of the Pitiusas Islands: carob, fig, almond and olive trees.

With regards to its fauna, of particular interest are its emblematic lizards, which are almost symbolic (no shop is complete without T-shirts or other clothes bearing their image). Indeed, when the Greeks called the island *Ophiousa Serpentaria* they were in fact referring to lizards rather than serpents (unlike one might expect, given the name), since the latter do not exist on the island.

The history of Formentera dates back to the Bronze Age: the megalithic monument in *Ca na Costa* dates back to around 1800 BC. The Romans named it *Frumentaria,* after the wheat fields that existed at the time, from which its current name derives.

After the Christian Reconquest, Guillem de Montgrí granted the island in fief to Berenguer Renart in 1246. The Augustinian monks founded the Monastery of Santa María in 1258.

Later, due to the constant risk of raids by Berber pirates, the island was left uninhabited for over 300 years, until the first stable settlement was established in 1726, with the founding of *Sant Francesc Xavier.* Nonetheless, throughout this

Espalmador island.

Cap de Barbària lighthouse.

Double page overleaf, view of Formentera from La Mola.

the only harbour for sports and recreational vessels, with around 150 berths. Near to the port, to the south, we find *S'Estany des Peix*, a natural bay with a narrow channel leading out to sea.

Further on, we find the remains of an 18th century watchtower at *Punta de sa Gavina*.

On the other side of the port, the northern side, there is another natural pool whose intense smell of salt and stagnant seaweed led to it being named *S'Sestany Pudent* (Putrid Pool). On one side, the salt pools, which are now practically unused, provide a perfect refuge for birds.

On both sides of the narrow peninsula formed by *Punta del Trucadors*, there lie the most famous and popular beaches of Las Pitiusas, *Illetes* and *Llevant*, huge expanses of sand which are bathed by crystal-clear waters and are entirely free of concrete. They are linked to the *island of S'Espalmador* by a narrow straight which can be crossed on foot at low tide. This small island possesses a small 18th century fortress called *Sa Torreta*.

If we follow the main road 3 km inland, we reach Sant Francesc Xavier, with its 1726 church-fortress which was even equipped with artillery (a couple of cannons), in order to defend itself from pirate attacks. Inside, it consists of a single nave with three sections and apse chapels in a rectangular alignment. This village has around 1000 inhabitants and contains the interesting *Ethnological Museum of Formentera*, with a display of everyday tools from the recent past. We continue to **Sant Ferran,** where we can visit an unusual church with unpainted walls. In the 1960s, many of the hippies who had settled on the island would meet in this town. In *Fonda Pepe* we can see a photo of Bob Dylan sat at one of its rustic tables, at the start of his career.

period, groups of workers constantly visited the island in order to maintain the land's crops and, above all, to exploit the saltworks which, together with fishing, were the only means of subsistence which existed prior to the development of tourism. Another two parishes were founded towards the end of the 18th century, *Sant Ferrán* and *El Pilar*, but it was not until the end of the 19th century that these were constituted as municipalities, together with the fishing village in the port of *La Savina*, totalling 2000 inhabitants in all.

We shall head inland from the port of La Savina, the only entrance for passenger boats from Ibiza and also

44

Estany des Peix.

Bicycles are the ideal form of transport on Formentera.

Just 2 km away, towards the coast, we find **Es Pujols,** currently the largest tourist destination on the island, whose beach is presided by another of the many watchtowers. To the south of Sant Francesc there is an area of desolate landscape, after which we reach *Cap de Barbária,* with a lighthouse and a defence tower, the *Torre des Garroveret.*
If we continue towards *La Mola* and turn off to the right, we find **Playa de Mitjorn,** another important tourist resort.

By ascending to the island's highest point, La Mola, one can enjoy a beautiful view of the whole island. Nearby stands the parish of *Nuestra Señora del Pilar,* a small Ibizan-style church.
The road ends at the impressive **lighthouse of La Mola,** at the top of a striking row of cliffs.

To the right, Cala Saona.

Festival in El Pilar de La Mola.

Windmill in El Pilar.

Craftwork.